50 ways to
stay
warm

Keep yourself cozy without breaking the bank

Alexandra Parsons

DOG 'n' BONE

For my children and their families who keep their homes at a planet-friendly 18°C. Thank you for the fleeces, jackets, scarves, and bed socks you provide when we visit.

Published in 2023 by Dog 'n' Bone Books
An imprint of Ryland Peters & Small Ltd
20–21 Jockey's Fields   341 E 116th St
London WC1R 4BW   New York, NY 10029

www.rylandpeters.com

10 9 8 7 6 5 4 3 2 1

Text and design © Dog 'n' Bone Books 2023
For illustrations copyright, see page 64.

A CIP catalog record for this book is available from the Library of Congress and the British Library.

ISBN: 978 1 912983 76 6

Printed in China

Design concept: Geoff Borin

Senior designer: Emily Breen
Art director: Sally Powell
Head of creative: Leslie Harrington
Head of production: Patricia Harrington
Publishing manager: Penny Craig

Contents

1

Stating
the obvious

"Freezers are good for preserving dead meat,
to preserve life we need a warm environment."

Abhijit Naskar

Exercise

Get moving! Running on the spot, jack jumps, push-ups... any kind of exercise will warm you up, with the added benefit of making you feel virtuous. That warm glow is partly from your halo but mainly from your muscles, busily burning calories and creating body heat. Give me another 50 press-ups and feel the burn.

Wear layers

Big thick sweaters and hefty overcoats may sound like a good idea at first... but

A) It is hard to pull off a killer style when all trussed up.

B) What to do if out and about and inevitably you warm up? Strip off and shiver?

Layers are the answer. Thin, thermal underwear would work for layer one, but so would something silky and provocative. Layer two should be insulating: a woolen sweater or a fleecy thing or maybe both. Top with a stylish windproof garment. Add a layer if still cold. Take off a layer if hot. Makes sense.

Eat warming foods

Cold bodies need calories to burn, but not necessarily from greasy, fried food. Here is a list of some warming foods. The challenge is to create a dish from these ingredients. Let's cook!

- Apples
- Bananas
- Coconuts
- Coffee
- Garlic
- Ginger
- Mangoes
- Nuts
- Oats
- Onions
- Oranges
- Red meat
- Spices—particularly hot ones like pepper, chili, cayenne, and turmeric
- Squash
- Sweet potato
- Tomatoes

Drink water

DO stay hydrated! It is important, because the body needs water to maintain temperature balance. In winter, all bundled up, it's harder to tell if you are sweating and, what with all that dry, heated air, you could start evaporating. So, a glass of cold water can keep you warm, but hot ginger tea might be altogether nicer...

Drink alcohol/ Don't drink alcohol

Aha! You may THINK a drink will warm you up on a cold night. That's because alcohol opens up the blood vessels in your skin (big, red drinker's nose ring a bell?) Your skin may feel warm, but those vital organs aren't getting enough blood and oxygen to function properly—you won't shiver quite so much, and shivering is designed to tell you to go back inside and get warm. And another thing: if you've had a skinful, you are more likely to do something foolish, like head out in a blizzard in your underwear or slip inadvertently under a snow plough.

Tumble dryer tip

While brushing your teeth and showering in the morning, bundle your clothes in the dryer for a short, hot tumble. There's nothing nicer than climbing into toasty, warm clothes.... The effect won't last, but what a splendidly warm way to start the day. Remember to empty your pockets first, though.

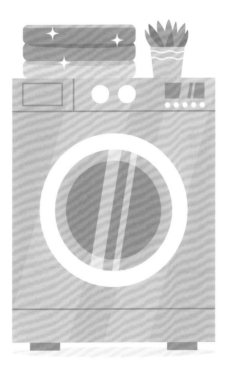

Wear heated clothing

There are gilets and vests and even leggings with heating elements that can raise your body temperature rather than just maintain it. Perfect if you work outdoors or in a refrigeration plant. But beware of getting hot and sweaty, as damp, heated leggings aren't very pleasant to wear. An added bonus is that these heated outfits come with a battery pack and charging outlet, so you can fire up your mobile phone at the same time as getting warm. How tech-savvy is that?

Keep extremities warm

All that folklore about losing a huge percentage of your body heat through your head isn't true. You lose as much as you would from anywhere else that was uncovered. But "hats on" makes sense. Your hands and feet also get chillier because blood rushes to your core to keep all those vital organs functioning in the cold, and rather abandons hands and feet to the ravages of frostbite. Always wear a hat, gloves, and warm socks if you're going out in the cold.

Warm the bed

Back in the day, bed-warming was a risky business involving servants, tongs, hot coals, and scalding hot copper warming pans. So, hurrah for the electric blanket: clean, simple… but still risky. Look up the statistics for fires and electrocutions by blanket and unplug. Consider the hot water bottle and the cosy bag of comforting wheat that you zap in the microwave—how safe are they? But a word to the wise: beware a combination of the two. Should the bottle leak and wet the warm grains, they will germinate, and you will lie in a soggy field of wheat till morning comes.

2

The science of warm

"There's really no such thing as 'cold,' when you're talking about the body, there's always heat—it's just a matter of keeping it in."

Richard Ingebretsen, MD, PhD

Be a man

One hesitates, in these woke times, to suggest that there are differences between men and women, but here goes: biologically, men have more muscle mass than women, and muscle is a natural heat producer. Women have roughly 10 percent more insulating body fat than men—it keeps their inner reproductive organs warm at the expense of blood carrying heat to the skin. So, a woman's body loses heat quicker than a man's. Fact.

Stop breathing

Not really a practical option—so don't try this at home—but as you breathe out, you lose heat. You are expelling air that has been warmed by your body, and then breathing in cold air which is obviously not going to warm you up any. (Dogs pant to keep cool!) The trick is to breathe in and out through the nose and, if that isn't working, wrap a scarf around your nose and mouth or wear a full-face balaclava—although you may get arrested for looking menacing.

Don't get sweaty

Evaporation is not a good thing. Getting hot and sweaty is quite easy to do if you are wearing too many clothes and moving around too much in the cold. The danger is that your wet and sweaty inner layer of clothing will wick warmth away from your body. Dry equals warm, so change out of those sweaty clothes immediately!

Trap your body heat

Radiation, or the transfer of heat, is the simple science behind trapping body heat with multiple layers of clothing and not letting it get away. Although there are smart, technical fabrics and clothing that will keep you dry and warm, they are quite expensive. Maybe fashioning cold-weather gear from bubble wrap would be more planet-friendly and have the same effect? Could catch on.

Slather on the Vaseline®

Convection is what is going on when cold air meets warm skin. Put simply, that would be Warm Skin: 0/Cold Air: 1. However, if the cold air has to battle through a thick, sticky layer of Vaseline® (petroleum jelly) to get at exposed parts of the face, then the score is Warm Skin: 1/Cold Air: 0.

Don't sit on an ice block

Common sense really, but the scientific term is conduction. If you sit or stand on a cold surface, guess what's going to happen? Heat always moves from the warmer object to the colder object and there is an equation for that. Just don't ask me to recall it.

Recognize the signs of hypothermia

Exhausted? Confused? Slurred speech? Blue lips? Breathing slowly? Numb extremities? Cold, dry skin? Weak pulse? Shivering? (Actually, shivering is a good sign that the body's heat regulation systems are still active; it's when the shivers stop that you need to call an ambulance.) Obviously, there are things you can and should do while you are waiting for the emergency services to pitch up, like move the person to a warm place,

insulate them from the cold ground, give them a warm drink, make sure they are dry, cover them with blankets, and sing a warm song such as:

Martha and the Vandellas, *Heat Wave*
Bruce Springsteen, *I'm on Fire*
Alicia Keys, *Girl on Fire*
Ed Sheeran, *I See Fire*

Actually, that could be very annoying; best to just murmur platitudes.

3

In the home

"Here's a winter tip for you for the next time the power grid gets knocked offline: wooden furniture is just decorative firewood."

Jarod Kintz

Spend more time upstairs

It's cozier up there! Heat rises so, in theory, in a centrally heated house the upstairs should be warmer than downstairs. Keep the windows shut and internal doors open so the downstairs heat can circulate. Try to resist the temptation to pull on bed socks and climb into bed.

Reverse the ceiling fan

This being the ceiling fan that you have installed to keep you cool in the blistering heat of summer. Who knew it could warm you up? Well, if you can get the fan to turn clockwise at a low speed, it will push the warm air that has (as every schoolkid knows) risen, back down to floor level where you might just feel the benefit.

Leave the bathroom door open

What to do with all that warm, moist air generated during a showering session? Share it with the rest of the house, of course. Leave the door open, shut off the fan, and let that humid, shower gel-scented air waft into the hallway, down the stairs, and out through the cat flap. Just don't do this if you have a smoke alarm outside your bathroom door—the warm vapor may set it off.

Leave the oven door open

Not all the time, obviously, but just after cooking. Don't shut in the residual heat, share it with the household. Peek in from time to time to make sure no babies or pets have crawled in.

Watch a roaring fire video

I know this works! Picture the scene... a very cold province of Canada in mid-winter (not there for the winter wonderland experience, but visiting relations). In a borrowed apartment, in an elderly block, with a central heating system that has "temporarily failed us folks!" Wearing all the clothing we had brought with us, clutching hot mugs of terrible coffee, we channel hop on the TV. And there it was: the famous *Burning Log* video on the Shaw cable channel—a continuous loop that runs all day with NO ADS! YAY!

Commission tapestries

Perhaps not something you would do every day, but back when owners of draughty medieval castles were figuring out how to deal with cold, stone walls, it was definitely an option. Nice, thick, woolen hangings with stories woven into them! How cozy and uplifting is that? Plus they are portable, for when you move house. You could replicate this practical and colorful medieval insulation solution by suspending colorful blankets or rugs from curtain poles or wires, not just round the walls but over windows too.

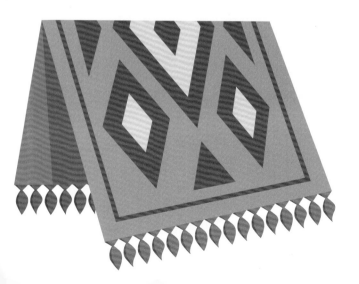

Wrap the windows

Not very lovely to look at, but a whole lot cheaper than double glazing. You do not have to wrestle with rolls of kitchen plastic wrap and those lethal cutting strips, however. Window insulation kits containing "secondary glazing film" and sticky tape are widely available. The installation may involve wetting the window and getting out the hairdryer—what to do if you get wrinkles, or inadvertently trap a spider, I hesitate to think.

Get tough on draughts

Cold wind whistling under the door or round rickety window frames can really mess with your heating bills. You can buy new windows and doors (expensive), fill every crack with ingenious specialist tapes (time-consuming), or add to your Instagramable winter decor and recycling kudos by making sausage-shaped draught excluders from old pantyhose or trouser legs filled with dried lentils, old socks, or plastic bags. What's not to love?

Hibernate

There is a sliver of evidence that some of our distant ancestors did hibernate (in layman's terms that's a physiological state of metabolic depression) and we may have, tucked away somewhere in our DNA, a gene or two that could be worked on so we could do it again. Useful for space travel, so they say, but also a pretty good way to get through winter.

"People don't notice if it is winter
or summer if they are happy."

Anton Chekhov

Picture credits

Gather round a light bulb

An inefficient incandescent light bulb emits 90% of its energy as heat. Admittedly it is a tiny heat source, and in the UK they have been phased out for fairly good reasons, as many a scorched lamp shade and burned-down house can attest. But if you still have one rattling round in the cupboard under the stairs, and all else fails.... Just remember you need foam to put out electrical fires, not water.

Sleep with animals

On the plus side, you are tapping into the body heat of your pets. On the minus side there are

hygiene and allergy issues. Long ago on chilly farmsteads, houses were built to accommodate over-wintering livestock on the lower floor. Their body heat (and we all know what heat does) would rise up through a hatch in the floor for the benefit of the humans on the floor above. I do not think you could replicate this ingenious use of a heat source with a couple of cats and a labradoodle.

Sleep with other people

Sleeping with people is a whole other ballgame. It is basically a good thing. Sleeping with someone you love and trust warms you up, reduces anxiety, lowers blood pressure, boosts the immune system, improves REM sleep generally, and increases happiness. Ahhhh!

In harsh climates whole families, along with passing guests, tend to bunk up together, so you get the body-heat bonus of a tribe. You also get multiple snorers, groaners, and farters. Probably a bit unpleasant when all is said and done.

4

If caught unawares... outdoors

"Be unprepared, that's my motto.
Be unprepared, and let life overwhelm you."

Marty Rubin

Keep your back to the wind

If you have somehow failed to wrap up for bad weather, or if a sudden wild wind springs a surprise, the best you can do to protect yourself is to keep your back to the wind and head to a place of shelter. This could be tricky if the place of shelter is in the path of the wind—just get in some practice running backward or sidewise.

Cozy up to a compost bin

Just remember to wear serious breathing apparatus and don't get too close, as the fumes can be lethally toxic. The astonishing thing about compost is how hot it can get—up to 122°F (50°C)—from gases released by plant-based stuff rotting away gently. But that's not all... temperatures can get so high that the pile of rot spontaneously bursts into flames. To be fair, that's quite rare, but quite warming.

Emergency insulation

First, select your newspaper—
broadsheets are best—then
crumple up the individual
sheets and stuff the paper
up your jumper and
down your trousers.
Why crumpled? Because
that way you create pockets of
air, which help retain body heat. All will
be well unless you get sweaty—damp
newspaper is for making paper maché, not for
adding warmth. Flattened out, a newspaper is
pretty useless as insulating material, but you
could always read the financial pages—maybe
come the next cold snap you will be able to
afford a fleecy jacket.

Places of shelter 1

The carcass of a recently deceased large animal

It has been known, and not just in the movies. Distasteful as it may be, an animal carcass will protect you from the wind and one's own trapped body heat would make the inside of the animal warmer than the outside air. However, there are many drawbacks; not least of these are the animal's internal bodily fluids and squishy decomposing organs, which could be very irritating. Then there is the likelihood of getting wolfed up along with the carcass as some starving scavenger's next meal. Perhaps just check the weather when leaving home next time.

Places of shelter 2
A snow hole

Here's how it is done: make a mound of snow as large as you possibly can. It needs to be at least 6—8ft (1.8—2.4m) high, and if you have set off without a spade, then you'll just have to use your hands. Go slowly with this bit, because if your clothes get sweaty you will freeze (see page 21). You then have to pack the snow down as best you can while you build your mound, which could be exhausting. Once you have your mound, let it sit for a bit to settle. Then dig yourself an entrance, crawl inside, and start hollowing it out, pushing the snow out through the entrance as you go. Keep the entrance clear of snow to let out carbon dioxide and as soon as the blizzard ceases, crawl out and get help. Let's face it, you should not have got yourself in this mess in the first place.

5

If desperate

"To shorten winter, borrow some money
due in spring."

WJ Vogel

Catch an overnight bus

Does it matter where you are going? Should you have packed a toothbrush? Do you care about getting back to where you started from? Such existential thoughts could keep you well occupied on a warm, long-distance coach ride to a new—if uncertain—beginning.

Wait in a waiting room

Spend the day in the warm. Pick a venue where you will be totally ignored by anybody in charge of anything. Top picks: passport or visa office, local government office, or the complaints or customer service department of any large organization. Bring a picnic and a good book.

All-night movie marathon

Find a nice, warm cinema showing something that's not too frightening, loud, or shouty. Something with subtitles and lots of enigmatic pauses, such as the films of Jean-Luc Godard, or a season of black-and-white Hollywood romances to soothe you toward dreamland. Andy Warhol's six-hour *Sleep* certainly won't keep you awake. Bring a pillow.

Hot spring!

Let the earth's hot core do the work. Photogenic steaming pools of turquoise water heated by cracks in the earth's crust or by volcanic magma... it sounds so elemental and free, so in touch with nature and everything that our planet can offer us. Mostly though, hot springs are to be found in luxurious tourist brochures and involve travel, probably restricted access, and always some kind of fee.

Hot job!

You will not be chilly for long working near a blast furnace, so look to the steel industry. Glass blowing is also a promisingly warm career, but does require skill... you wouldn't want to breathe in when you should be blowing out, and there's an art to that. There are not many openings for shoveling coal into a steam engine, except on heritage steam engine lines. On a more relaxing level, how about becoming a sauna bath attendant? Harrogate Council are apparently desperate to find people to work in the municipal Turkish baths. Apply now!

Fire!

Join a society or a movement that likes making fires out of doors and let them do the work. Woodcraft Folk and Scouts and Guides are really good at laying fires and keeping them burning, but you may have to join in with the jolly, wholesome activities. Fire has an elemental pull and is also associated with some quite wicked things like burning books, torching dwellings, and pillaging. So do check on the ideology of any group you join. You will know you are in the wrong place if the "leader" gives you a pointy hat and a torch of your own.

Tips from those in the know

"The wisdom of the wise and the experience of the ages are perpetuated by quotations."

Benjamin Disraeli

Build an igloo

Unlike a hastily pushed-together snow hole (see page 42), an igloo is a triumph of ingenuity and simple science based on living in balance with one's surroundings. Up above the Arctic Circle, this means snow and ice and not much else. Let's face it, it's unlikely you will find yourself stranded in the Arctic with only this book to guide you, but if you are the kind of person who goes on unadvisable hikes in snowy wildernesses and forgets to bring a tent, you'll be glad you read on.

Do bring a saw with you, as you'll need to cut bricks from crusty snow. First mark out a circle, cut a layer of snow bricks from within the circle, and put to one side. Now dig a trench down to the ground in the center—the raised parts on each side will be sleeping platforms, and the trench will lead to the entrance, which must be as low down as possible for better heat retention. Next, build the walls using the snow bricks and make sure they are packed together tightly. Curve the walls inward until you have a lovely, smooth, domed shape, leaving a ventilation hole somewhere in the ceiling. You might wish to add a porch. Cover the sleeping platform with leaves and bits of forest debris. Good luck.

Make a fire in your igloo

Making a fire in an igloo needs some serious skills and familiarity with that equation about losing heat to colder air (see page 21). The fire must be in the center, far from the walls, and there must be a smoke hole at the top of the igloo. As the fire delivers heat to the ice inside the igloo, the ice itself loses heat to the colder air outside. So long as you get the balance right, your igloo won't melt.

$q = (U \times A) \times \Delta t$, if that is any help.

Make a tepee

If your surroundings turn out to be not snow and ice but endless chilly, windswept plains with grazing buffalo and the odd stand of trees, then nature dictates you build a tepee. First prepare your materials: chop down some tall trees to make tent poles, cure a few buffalo hides, and braid strips of one of the hides to make a load of ropes. Lash three long and sturdy poles together and stand the tripod firmly on the ground. Add a few more poles to the tripod to form a circle, lashing them in well, then stretch your buffalo hides around the poles using ropes to haul them into position. And don't forget to fashion smoke flaps. This is not so much a two-person job as a job for an entire tribe. OR you could use a tarpaulin, some lightweight aluminum tent poles, and some sturdy string.

All fur and no underpants

When the temperature really drops, you need some Arctic know-how. The Inuit and Yupik peoples fashion clothing from the skin of furry animals such as the caribou (not polar bears, they save those heavy skins for rugs). Best practice is to sew two hides together, the inner with fur next to the skin, and the outer with fur on the outside. This makes wind-proof, insulated clothing that far outperforms any super-techno kit yet invented. That's it! Top tip is not to wear any underwear, which would get sweaty and therefore wet and therefore cold. Fur traps body heat, which swirls comfortingly around inside your trousers and your anorak*.

* From the Greenlandish *annoraaq*, referring to a hooded pull-over jacket.

A travel tip

Traditional Arctic clothing was far from dull, decorated with seal-skin inserts, embroidery, feathers, fringes, and contrasting fur trims. The clothing had no pockets, but there was a particular style of baggy trouser, sewn to the boots for long journeys, that had space inside for keeping food warm, and storing other travel necessities. Here's a thought—could this be a way round those pesky airline baggage allowances?

Hot rocks!

Heat is not to be wasted. Build a fire outside your tent or tepee (inside if you are brave enough and have mastered the smoke-flap thing) and surround it with stones or bricks. When the fire has died down, the rocks will be warm! Wrap them up in a handy cloth and slip them inside your sleeping bag.

Fire on the move

Ponder the importance of fire out in the wilderness when no one had yet invented the match or the lighter. Fire is not only for keeping warm and cooking sausages, but also an element imbued with significance. For the Native American, it was important to take the same fire from camp to camp, and to keep the coals glowing with possibilities while packing up and traveling.
A buffalo horn carried over the shoulder in a harness was the answer. Consider using a bucket to carry your own sacred glow from place to place.

Rolling naked in the snow

Do not attempt this if you have a heart condition. However, getting very cold very quickly will get the blood rushing about your body. You will shiver, which will warm you up a bit and, as long as you can relax and breathe calmly, you should be able to support the cold for a short while before rushing indoors and jumping about to get warm and dry. Normally (if you could call this normal) snow-rolling is done in conjunction with a sauna— the heat and cold combo are designed to get the blood flowing and give you a warm, healthy glow. People who live in very cold climates have learned that it is not advisable to spend the entire winter lethargically wrapped up in front of a fire. Get out there and get cold!

Don't wear glasses

Another bulletin from the Department of Common Sense. This is something the inhabitants of Siberia have learned through experience—in extreme cold, do not go outside wearing glasses, as they will freeze to your face.

A Siberian heating system

Not surprisingly, heating systems in the coldest areas of Russia are government controlled and usually operate between September and May. The householder has no control over this whatsoever. A central station pumps out hot water to radiators in each home on the circuit via insulated underground pipes. What could possibly go wrong??